who's your daddy?

who's your daddy?

tim, phyllis & bob
MikWright, Ltd.

**Andrews McMeel
Publishing**

Kansas City

who's your daddy?

www.mikwright.com

02 03 04 05 RDS 10 9 8 7 6 5 4 3 2

ISBN: 0-7407-1410-4

Library of Congress Catalog Card Number: 00-108474

─────── attention: schools and businesses ───────

Andrews McMeel books are available at quantity
discounts with bulk purchase for educational, business,
or sales promotional use. For information, please write to:
Special Sales Department, Andrews McMeel Publishing,
4520 Main Street, Kansas City, Missouri 64111.

we dedicate *who's your daddy?*
to the many father figures in our lives,
and to those who used to be men.

acknowledgments

who's your daddy? is more of the same MikWright deadpan goofery. less than serious, tim and phyllis continue to bastardize family and friends while reaffirming their desire to consume cheap wine.

and now . . . meet bob, our in-house half-wit, searching for the recognition he never got in prison. anything you find offensive probably came from bob, our very own social deviant.

to scottie and terri:
can't you two get along? don't make us stop this car!

to kent, danny, dude, and bessie:
leona and barbara said they like us best.

to b.m.:
not every card can be about bodily functions,
thank you!

who's your daddy?

. . . in your wildest dreams!

meet melvin. what father of four midwestern farm girls wouldn't love to go to work as a prison guard? and what man wouldn't take advantage of this photo by hanging it prominently over the water fountain? that's quite a piece of artillery, mel!

lake norman was a wonderful spot to ponder
the past and to "let" a silent killer if you
so happened to be downwind.

hey willard . . . gettin' any?

i mean, catchin' any?

cecil! you didn't use protection?

howard boasted that he had a lot of
experience under his belt.
frankly, he never measured up.

uncle howard was one of six boys (twelve total children). howie is a progressive farmer always looking to conjure up the latest farming miracle. but then, there is pressure, since his brother invented the merry-go-round seen at every k-mart in america.

my earliest memories of uncle howie revolve around him spitting tobacco and saving a calf from the manure pit by walking out on water skis.

oh, for god's sake edgar, roll down
the window!

the right hand doesn't know what the left hand
is doing. it if did, it would be jealous.

he may have been a war hero alright,
but he never had the guts to buy the old lady
a box of tampons.

i should have known better than to ask for
a doggie bag at a chinese restaurant.

i was just three when i met my uncle roy's
roommate william. dad still calls him
"$3 bill."

you're kidding! i get both nipples?

o.k. then, it's settled.

a case of plutonium for a case of beer.

you can see trouble brewing.
in 1967, wes (in the striped shirt that he
still wears) looks as though he's conducting
international diplomacy with the italian
consulate. in actuality, phyllis's dad was
working on a plan to get pizza delivered to
the military base in thirty minutes or less.

many scientists believe that the
brontosaurus could consume up to three tons
of vegetation a day.

that's a lot of crap!

when fully erect . . . it would stop traffic.

i'll say one thing about ed . . .
when it comes to gas, he's always got it.

come on kitten!

we've never done it in a cathedral.

hurry up and take the damn picture, lillian!
they're going to run out of shrimp
on the buffet!

oh the memories . . .

grandma used to say "when i was your age,
i used to dance." then she would raise her
frail little arms over her head and gently
sway them from side to side, dancing to
music only she heard.

. . . oh the prescription drugs.

seven swans a swimming,

six geese a laying . . .

(make that three geese a laying)

the investigation concluded there was seaman
on the car.

so i called mavis to tell her i got eight
inches last night and, of course, the bitch
claimed she got nine.

i had the whole thing planned. when the snowplow would roar by, i was going to stand alongside the road and get smothered by the soft snow. i positioned myself for maximum coverage. with the snowplow approaching, i noticed the driver frantically waving to me as i ever-so-graciously waved back in anticipation of the thrill.

thrown halfway across the yard, winded, face stinging from the ice chunks, i realized my plan had flaws. to this day, nightmares of heavy snowfalls haunt my existence.
i moved south.

(and of course i did the "tongue on the metal" trick that same year.)

the gals were left alone whilst gary and
ronnie went to the boat show. they loved
their husbands . . . and everyone else's too,
for they were whores.

feeling a little anal?

who's gonna tell santa about prancer?

now sweetheart, i'm only saying that your
sister shouldn't spend so much on the kids
when she could be using that money
on electrolysis.

from the beginning of time, man has tried to manage body hair . . . lips, moles, and backs. recently a friend told us about the time he grabbed his wife's nair, thinking it was mousse. soon after, while at a holiday party, the burning sensation began. with clumps of hair falling into the shrimp cocktail, the party ended abruptly. bald is beautiful!

when emmett reached the peak, he got off.

sit down frank!

you don't know what you stand for.

ernest was mesmerized by the
size of clara's zinnias.

you should see the stud that bucked me
saturday night!

now if you kids can't stand still,
i'm going to call the prison and
tell your father!

while danny went on to become an eagle scout,
timmy went on to date one.

how i got messed up in scouting is beyond me.
we would meet after school in the catholic
church. as a lutheran, i was most fascinated
with the water trough in the foyer of the
chapel, which did not earn me a badge,
i assure you.

after a year of playing tag in the church
basement, i decided scouting was not for me.
my time would be better spent making
rhubarb pies with mom.

hank,

i've got to know your secret! how do you get
your pie crust so flaky?

ladies and gentlemen . . . we'd like to
welcome you to alabama. please set your
watches back six years.

finally, mr. right.

(or at least mr. right now)

clark was handsome, no he was pretty.
with that porcelain skin and kind nature and
a flair for gourmet cooking; well, we all said
a silent prayer for marlene.

about the authors . . . and bob.

tim and phyllis are sick. they both work from
the yet unknown parts of the brain. tim,
originally from rural minnesota, left the
family farm two days after graduation and
never looked back, except for an occasional
visit to collect rhubarb. phyllis lived the
fancy life. italy when young, east tennessee
as a teenager, and currently deciding whether
or not to pursue a second career as a natural
sugar consultant. should we ever run out of
espresso, phyllis gets her own office.

. . . and bob. you can never have enough smart asses in a grungy, by-the-railroad, fixed-up warehouse. that's what we thought. after a brisk, routine workout, bob saunters into the office for a café crème. bob's innate wit fits right in . . . but we have forbidden him from wearing his favorite leopard skin thong in the office.